Little Hands Story Bible

Carine
Mackenzie

Illustrated by
Jennifer
Stevenson

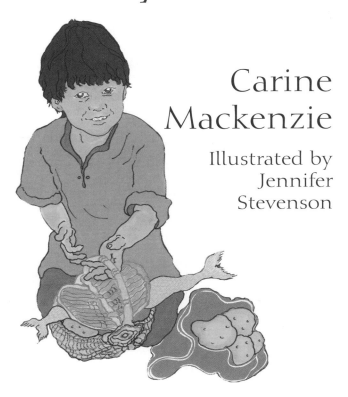

CHRISTIAN FOCUS PUBLICATIONS

Little Hands Story Bible

Before you read what God has to say to you
pray that He will teach you from his word as He
has promised. Ask Him to instruct you and
teach you in the way that you should go.
Ask Him to show you how wonderful He is and
how much you need Him.

© Copyright 1998 Carine Mackenzie
illustrated by Jennifer Stevenson
Published by Christian Focus Publications, Geanies
House, Fearn, Tain, Ross-shire, IV20 1TW, Scotland, U.K.
Web Page: www.christianfocus.com
email: info@christianfocus.com
This Paperback Edition 2001 ISBN 1-85792-697-8
reprinted 2003
Hardback Edition ISBN 1-85792-342-1
reprinted 2003
Printed in China

Stories from the Old Testament

Stories from the New Testament

Stories from the
Old Testament

God made the world

God made the whole world from nothing. He said, 'Let there be light,' and light appeared. He spoke again and water appeared. He spoke again and the land was made. He made plants and trees, the sun, moon and stars, and the birds, fish, and animals. He made all this in six days. Everything that God made was very good.

What did God make the world from?
God made all sorts of creatures. Which ones can you see in the picture?
Story found in Genesis chapter 1

God made people

On the sixth day God also made the first man. He was called Adam. God made him from the dust of the ground. God breathed life into Adam and he became alive.

God did not want Adam to be alone so he made a woman called Eve to be his wife. God made Eve from one of Adam's ribs.

How did God make Adam?
Can you see two creatures that fly in this picture?
Story found in Genesis chapter 2

Garden of Eden

Adam and Eve lived in the beautiful Garden of Eden. There were lovely trees there with good fruit to eat. Adam's job was to look after the garden. He gave names to all the animals and birds. God was their friend.

God allowed Adam and Eve to eat any of the fruit in the garden except for one special tree in the middle of the garden - the tree of the knowledge of good and evil.

What was Adam's job?
What colours are in the butterfly?
Story found in Genesis chapter 2

Sin spoils God's world

One day in the garden, Satan came, looking like a serpent and spoke to Eve. 'Did God really say you should not eat the fruit of the special tree?' 'Yes,' said Eve. 'If we do we will die.' 'That's not true,' said Satan.

Eve believed Satan. She took some of the fruit and gave some to Adam too. They both sinned by disobeying God. They were sent away from the garden as a punishment.

What did Adam and Eve do wrong?
What animal is on the tree?
Story found in Genesis chapter 3

Noah builds the Ark

People in the world were very bad. God decided to send a flood to destroy all the wicked people. He warned good Noah and told him to build a big boat for himself, his wife and his three sons and their wives.

They did what God told them and built the ark of wood, with a window and a door. The ark had three decks - plenty of room for Noah and his family and at least two of every animal.

Why did God send a flood?
What animals can you see in the picture?
Story found in Genesis chapter 6 & 7

Rainbow promise

Noah and his family were kept safe in the ark until the rain had stopped and the flood water had gone back down again. God told Noah to come out of the ark with his wife and family and all the animals.

God made the beautiful rainbow in the sky, as a sign of his promise, never to flood the whole earth again.

What promise did God make to Noah?
Point to the rainbow. What colours can you name?
Story found in Genesis chapter 8 & 9.

Abraham

Abraham and his wife Sarah lived in a land far away. God spoke to Abraham and told him to go on a long journey to another country. God promised to look after him. Abraham did as God asked.

God promised to bless him and his children. A baby boy called Isaac was born when Abraham and Sarah were very old. God kept his promise to them.

What was the name of Abraham and Sarah's baby boy?
How many people are in this picture?
Story found in Genesis chapters 12-21

A wife for Isaac

Abraham's servant was sent back to his home country to find a wife for Isaac. He made the long journey with ten camels.

He went to the well at evening time when the young women came to get water. The servant asked one young woman to give him a drink. This kind girl gave the servant a drink at once and also brought water for his camels. The girl was called Rebekah. She went back with the servant to become Isaac's wife.

What was Isaac's wife called?
How many camels can you see?
Story found in Genesis chapter 24

The Twins

Isaac and Rebekah had twin sons called Jacob and Esau. Sometimes twins look very like each other. Jacob and Esau were completely different.

Esau was red and his skin was hairy. Jacob's skin was smooth.

Esau loved hunting wild animals out in the country while Jacob liked to stay near home.

Which twin loved hunting?
What is Jacob holding in this picture?
Story found in Genesis chapter 25 verses 1-34

Joseph's special coat

Joseph had eleven brothers, but his father loved him best. His father gave him a lovely coat with many beautiful colours. His brothers were upset.

Joseph had two dreams. The meaning of the dreams was that Joseph would be more important than his brothers. The brothers disliked him all the more.

Why did the brothers not like Joseph?
Look at Joseph's coat - how many colours can you name?
Story found in Genesis chapter 37 verses 1-11

Joseph goes to Egypt

One day Joseph's father sent him to find out how his brothers were. They were in the country looking after the sheep. When they saw him coming they made a plan to get rid of him. They put Joseph in a deep pit.

When some travellers came along, they sold Joseph as a slave for twenty pieces of silver. He was sent to Egypt. The boys then tricked their father, to make him believe Joseph was dead.

How much was Joseph sold for?
What is inside the man's bag?
Story found in Genesis chapter 37 verses 12-36

Joseph helps his brothers

God helped Joseph through all his hard times. He was a slave and had to work very hard. Then he was thrown into prison - a wicked woman told lies about him. God was still with him.

Because Joseph told the King the meaning of a dream, he was given an important job looking after the grain crops. Many years later men from a far off land came to buy food from Joseph. They were his brothers.

Who helped Joseph all the time?
What colours is Joseph wearing in this picture?
Story found in Genesis chapters 39-45

Baby in the basket

Pharaoh, King of Egypt, was cruel. He hated God's people and wanted all the baby boys killed. One mother and father bravely made a plan to save their baby. They made a basket of rushes and placed the baby inside. As it floated in the river, it was watched by his big sister.

The baby was found by the Princess who kept him for her own son, but she asked the mother to be his nurse. She called him Moses.

How was the baby kept safe?
What colour are the rushes in the river?
Story found in Exodus chapters 1-2

The Burning Bush

Moses was looking after the sheep in the desert. He saw a bush on fire, but the bush did not burn up. How strange! Moses went nearer to see better.

God spoke to him from the bush. 'Do not come any closer. Take off your shoes. You are standing on holy ground.' Moses was afraid. 'I am sending you to rescue my people from slavery,' said God. 'I will be with you.'

What was Moses told to take off?
Can you see Moses' shoes?
Story found in Exodus chapter 3 verses 1-14

The Red Sea

The people of Israel left the land of Egypt where they had been slaves. Moses was their leader, helped by his brother Aaron. God showed them where to go.

A pillar of cloud led them in the day and a pillar of fire at night. When they came to the Red Sea, God caused the sea to part and a dry road was made for them right through the sea. The people of Israel left the land of Egypt where they had been slaves. Moses was their leader. Everyone crossed safely.

How did God help his people get across the sea? What is Moses holding in his hand? Story found in Exodus chapter 14

Manna

God gave food to the people as they travelled across the desert. Every morning God covered the ground with small white seeds called manna. The people collected this, crushed it and then made cakes with it. The people gathered just enough for that day. On the day before the Sabbath they were given enough for two days.

What was the name of the food God sent?
How many children are in this picture?
Story found in Numbers chapter 11 verses 4-9

Water from the rock

There was no water in the desert and the people were thirsty. They grumbled to Moses and Aaron. Moses and Aaron prayed to God. God said to Moses, 'Gather the people together. Speak to that rock and water will pour out of it.'

All the people came to Moses. He hit the rock twice with his stick. Water poured out. All the people and the animals had enough to drink.

How did Moses get water from the rock?
How many birds can you see in this picture?
Story found in Numbers chapter 20 verses 1-13

The Ten Commands

God called Moses to the top of Mount Sinai. He gave him ten commandments for the people to follow. The commands were written on two big stones by God.

Jesus summed up the commands like this - you should love God with all your heart, soul, strength and mind. You should love your neighbour as yourself. We should obey these commandments too.

What did Jesus say?
How many stones is Moses holding in this picture?
Story found in Exodus chapter 20 verses 1-17

Joshua

Joshua and the people marched on to Jericho. The walls were high. The gates were tightly shut. But God was with them. He told them what to do. 'March round Jericho for six days.'

Round and round they marched, with the priests blowing their trumpets. On the seventh day they marched round seven times. Everyone shouted loudly. The big strong walls fell down flat. Joshua and the people of Israel had won the battle of Jericho. God had helped them.

How did the walls fall down?
What are the people waving in the picture?
Story found in Joshua chapter 6 verses1-20

Gideon

Gideon had lots of soldiers in his army. 'Your army is too big.' said God, 'you think you do not need my help.'

Lots of men decided to go home. 'Your army is *still* too big. Tell the men to take a drink from the river.'

The men who took the water up to their mouths with their hands were the ones who were chosen. Gideon and his small army won the battle with God's help.

Who helped Gideon win the battle?
Where are the men drinking from in the picture?
Story found in Judges chapter 7

Ruth and Naomi

Ruth's mother-in-law, Naomi wanted to go back to her home land - to Bethlehem. Both women were widows; their husbands had died.

Ruth decided to go with Naomi. 'Do not ask me to leave you,' she said. 'I want to go where you go. Your people will be my people and your God will be my God.' How glad Naomi would be to have Ruth with her.

Where was Naomi's home town?
How many women are in this picture?
Story found in Ruth chapter1

Ruth and Boaz

Ruth went out to the fields to gather up any grain that the workers had dropped. She went to Boaz's field.

Boaz was very kind to her. 'Drop some grain on purpose,' he told his workers, 'so that Ruth can gather plenty to take home to Naomi.'

Naomi was so pleased when Ruth came home with a large amount of grain.

Whose field did Ruth gather grain from ?
What colour is Ruth's dress in this picture?
Story found in Ruth chapter 2

Birth of Samuel

Hannah was very sad because she did not have any children. She wanted to have a baby very much. She went to the House of God and prayed that God would give her a baby boy. God answered her prayer.

Some time later she had a baby boy of her own. She called him Samuel, which means, 'asked of God', because she had prayed to God for this baby boy.

What does the name Samuel mean?
In this picture is the baby awake or asleep?
Story found in 1 Samuel chapter 1 verses 1-20

God calls Samuel

One night Samuel was lying in bed in the temple. He heard a voice calling his name, 'Samuel.'

'Here I am' he called back running through to Eli.
'I did not call you,' Eli replied.
'Go back to bed.'

After hearing the voice three times, Samuel knew that it was God speaking to him. 'Speak Lord for your servant is listening' he said. God spoke to Samuel.

What did Samuel say to God?
Can you point to the candle in this picture?
Story found in 1 Samuel chapter 3

David the Shepherd

David was a shepherd boy who looked after his father's sheep. He worked out on the hillside taking the sheep to find food and water. He was very brave.

Once a lion and a bear came to steal a lamb. David caught them both and rescued the lamb. God looked after David and kept him safe.

Who looked after David?
What is David looking after in this picture?
Story found in 1 Samuel chapter 17 verses 34-36

David the fighter

Goliath was a wicked giant who fought against the people of Israel. 'I will fight against Goliath' said young David. 'God will help me.'

He took five smooth stones and his shepherd's sling and faced up to the big giant. David aimed one stone which hit Goliath right in the forehead. He fell down dead. David had saved his people from the enemy.

What did David use to fight Goliath?
Can you see the stones that David has found?
Story found in 1 Samuel chapter 17

Queen of Sheba

The Queen of Sheba heard how wise King Solomon was. She wanted to find out for herself if this was really true. She travelled a great distance to Solomon's palace. She arrived with camels carrying gifts - spices, gold, and jewels. She asked Solomon lots of hard questions and he answered them all. Nothing was too hard for him to explain. When she went home, she knew that Solomon was very wise.

What presents did the Queen of Sheba bring to Solomon?
What animal can you see in this picture?
Story found in 1 Kings chapter 10 verses 1-13

Fed by the birds

For a long time there was no rain, which meant that the crops could not grow. Elijah, the man of God was hungry and thirsty. God told him where to go to get a drink from a little river. So Elijah had water to drink.

'I have told some birds called ravens to bring food for you,' God told Elijah. The ravens brought bread and meat to Elijah, every morning and every evening.

Who brought food to Elijah?
What is in the bird's beak?
Story found in 1 Kings chapter 17 verses 1-7

Plenty to eat

A mother went out to gather sticks to make a fire. There was hardly any food in the land. She was going to have some bread with her last drop of oil and flour, when she met Elijah, the man of God.

'Bake me a cake first,' he said. 'God will provide enough for you and your boy.'

The jar of oil did not run dry and the bin of flour was not used up. The lady, her son and Elijah had plenty to eat.

What did the lady use to make the bread?
Who is the youngest person in this picture?
Story found in 1 Kings chapter 17 verses 8-16

Naaman

Naaman was a brave soldier, but he had a horrible disease, called leprosy. The little servant girl said to Naaman's wife, 'If only my master could see the man of God in my home country, he would make him better.'

Naaman went to see Elisha, the man of God. He told him to wash in the river Jordan. His leprosy was cured. How happy the little servant girl must have been.

What was wrong with Naaman?
Look at the picture and you will see what Naaman was told to do.
Story found in 2 Kings chapter 5 verses 1-15

Nehemiah builds the Walls

The walls of Jerusalem had been broken down. Nehemiah was sad to hear this. He asked his master the King of Persia, if he could go back to build up the walls again. The King said, 'Yes.'

What a huge task for Nehemiah! Many people made fun of him and even tried to stop the work. But God helped Nehemiah. The wall was finished in only fifty two days.

What did Nehemiah build with God's help?
What colour is Nehemiah's coat?
Story found in Nehemiah chapters 1-6

The Lions' Den

Daniel loved God. He prayed to him often. Some bad men did not like Daniel. They made the King make a bad law - anyone who prayed to God was to be put into a den of lions.

Daniel prayed as usual. He was put into the lions' den. But God kept him safe, the lions did not hurt him.

Who kept Daniel safe in the lions' den?
How many lions can you see in this picture?
Story found in Daniel chapter 6

Jonah runs aw

God told Jonah to go to a c y,
far away to tell people about
him. Jonah was afraid and
sailed away in a boat. A big
storm came. The other sailors
threw Jonah into the sea, but
he did not drown. God sent a
large whale to swallow Jonah.

Jonah was put out by the
whale on dry land. Then he did
what God had asked him to
do.

How did Jonah reach dry land?
Can you find Jonah in this picture?
Story found in Jonah chapters 1-4

Stories from the New Testament

The birth of Jesus

One day an angel came to visit Mary. 'You are going to have a very special baby,' he told her. 'Do not be afraid. You shall call his name Jesus.' Mary was amazed at this news. How could that happen?
'Your baby is the Son of God,' said the angel.

Mary's baby was born while she was visiting Bethlehem. There was no room in the inn. The special baby was born in a stable and laid to sleep in a manger.

In what building was the baby Jesus born?
Who is the lady in this picture?
Story found in Luke chapter 1and chapter 2.

Shepherds in the fields

Some shepherds were out in the fields one night taking care of their sheep. An angel came to them with great news. 'Today in the town of Bethlehem the Saviour has been born.'

The shepherds hurried to Bethlehem and found baby Jesus lying in a manger. The shepherds praised God for the birth of this baby. They told the good news to everyone they met.

In which town was Jesus born?
Can you find the lamb in the picture?
Story found in Luke chapter 2 verses 8-20

The Wise Men

Wise men from an Eastern county came to look for Jesus. They had seen a special star in the sky.

They wanted to meet the new king that had been born. They followed the star. It led them to where Jesus was. They brought lovely presents for the baby - gold and incense and myrrh. They bowed down and worshipped Jesus.

Who were the wise men looking for?
Where is the star?
Story found in Matthew chapter 2 verses 1-12

Jesus grows up

Jesus grew up in the town of Nazareth with his family. Joseph was a carpenter who made things from wood. Jesus' mother was called Mary. He had several brothers and sisters. Jesus grew strong and healthy and wise. He was like no other child. He did not do anything wrong. He always did what God wanted him to do.

What was Joseph's work?
How many people are in this picture?
Story found in Luke chapter 2 verses 39-40

Jesus in Jerusalem

When Jesus was twelve years old, he went with his parents to Jerusalem for a special feast. Crowds came from all over the country. On the way home Mary and Joseph realised that Jesus was missing. They rushed back to Jerusalem to look for him. At last they found Jesus in the temple, speaking with the wise teachers.

'Did you not know that I had to be in my Father's house,' he said. He was meaning God, his Father.

Where did Mary and Joseph find Jesus?
Do Mary and Joseph look happy or sad?
Story found in Luke chapter 2 verses 41-52

Simon Peter

Simon was a fisherman on the sea of Galilee. One day his brother Andrew told him good news about Jesus. 'He is the one sent by God to take away the sins of the world,' said Andrew.

Andrew took his brother Simon to meet Jesus. Jesus asked Simon and Andrew to follow him and be among his twelve disciples. Jesus gave Simon a new name - he called him Peter.

Who took Simon to meet Jesus?
Can you find the boats on the water?
Story found in John chapter 1 verses 35-42

The wedding

Jesus and his mother and his friends were guests at a wedding. In the middle of the party, Jesus' mother came to him and said, 'They have no more wine.' She was sure he could help.

Jesus told the servants to fill up six big pots with water. Jesus then turned the water into the very best wine.

Who turned the water into wine?
How many pots of water can you see?
Story found in John chapter 2 verses 1-11

Wise and foolish builders

Jesus told a story about two men who were building a house. The wise man built his house on a rock. It was firm and strong. When the rain and winds came, the house was safe.

The foolish man built his house on sand. When the rain and wind came, his house came crashing down and was washed away. 'The wise person listens to God's word and lives by it,' Jesus said.

Whose house stood firm?
Where is the broken house?
Where is the strong house?
Story found in Matthew chapter 7 verses 24-27

Four good friends

A poor, lame man lay on his mat all day long. He couldn't walk. He had four good friends. 'Let's take our friend to Jesus,' they said. So they carried him on his mat to the house where Jesus was but because of the crowds of people, they could not get in.

They climbed up the outside stair, opened up the roof and lowered their friend down in front of Jesus. 'Your sins are forgiven,' said Jesus. 'Take your mat and go home.' The man was cured.

Where did the friends take the lame man?
How many people are in the picture?
Story found in Mark chapter 2 verses 1-12

The Farmer

Jesus told a story about a farmer sowing the seed. Some seed fell on the path and birds ate it up. Some fell on the rocky ground and it soon died. Some fell among the thorns and the plant soon died.

But some fell on good ground and it grew well and gave a good harvest. If we listen to Jesus' words and obey them, that is like the good seed.

What happened to the seed that fell on the path?
Can you see the birds hiding by the rocks?
Story found in Matthew chapter 13 verses 1-9

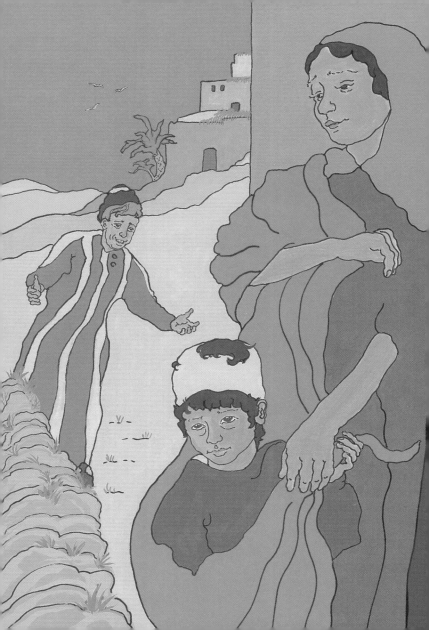

The sick boy

An important man from Capernaum had a little boy who was very sick. 'Please come to see my son before he dies,' the father begged Jesus.

'Your son will live,' Jesus replied. 'Go back home.'

The father believed Jesus. Before he reached home, his servant came running to meet him. 'Your son is better.' He had got better at the exact time that Jesus had spoken to his father.

What good news did the servant bring?
What is wrapped around the boy's head?
Story found in John chapter 4 verses 46-54

Pool of Bethesda

Around the pool of Bethesda were many people who could not see or walk.

One man had been there for a long, long time. He had no friend to help him.

'Do you want to get better?' asked Jesus. 'Get up, pick up your mat and walk.' At once the man was better. He picked up his mat and walked off.

Who made the lame man better?
What are the people sitting beside?
Story found in John chapter 5 verses 1-9

Calming the storm

Jesus and his friends went out in a boat across the lake of Galilee. Jesus fell asleep. A storm suddenly blew up and waves swept over the boat. The friends were afraid and woke Jesus. He got up and spoke to the wind and the waves.

'Quiet! Be still!' At once, all was calm. His friends were so amazed by Jesus' power.

How did Jesus calm the waves?
Is the water calm or stormy in the picture?
Story found in Mark chapter 4 verses 35-41

Jesus loves Children

Jesus loves little children. Little children were brought by their parents to Jesus so that he would put his hand on them and pray for them.

The disciples tried to turn them away but Jesus said, 'Let the little children come to me. Don't stop them. The Kingdom of heaven belongs to them and those like them.'

Was Jesus pleased to see little children?
How many children are in the picture?
Story found in Matthew chapter 19 verses 13-15

Jairus' daughter

Jairus' little girl was very ill. Jairus went to find Jesus to ask him to make her well. By the time Jesus came to her house the little girl had died.

Jesus went into her room with her mother and father and his friends John, James and Peter. He said to the little girl - 'get up!' She sat up in bed. Jesus had made her better. 'Give her something to eat,' Jesus said.

What did Jesus say to the little girl?
What is the little girl doing in the picture?
Story found in Luke chapter 8 verses 40-56

The kind man

A poor man lay badly hurt on a lonely road. He had been robbed and beaten up. One man came along, but he hurried past. Then another man came; he looked but hurried on too.

Then a kind man came along on his donkey. He felt so sorry for the poor man. He bandaged his wounds, then put him on his donkey and took him to an inn where he looked after him. Jesus tells us to be like the kind man.

What did the kind man do?
What animal can you see in this picture?
Story found in Luke chapter 10 verses 25-37

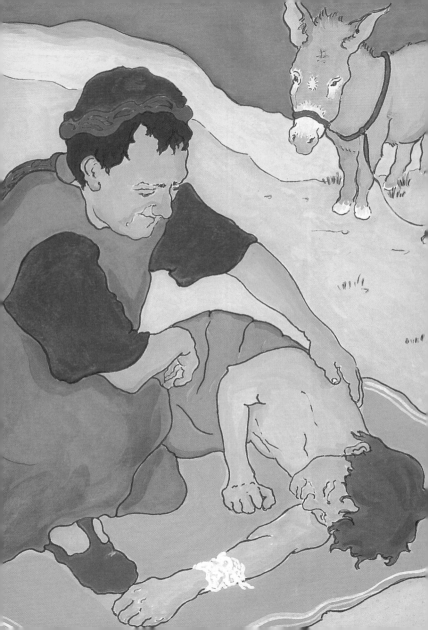

Mary and Martha

Mary and Martha were sisters who were friends of Jesus. Jesus would often go to their house for a meal.

One day Martha was busy cooking, while Mary sat listening to Jesus. Martha complained to Jesus. 'Why is Mary leaving me to do all the work?'

'Don't be so worried about serving the supper,' said Jesus. 'Mary is right to spend the time listening to me.'

Which sister loved to sit and listen to Jesus?
How many bowls can you see in this picture?
Story found in Luke chapter 10 verses 38-42

Lazarus

Mary and Martha's brother, Lazarus became very sick. The sisters sent for Jesus, but before he came, Lazarus died. Mary and Martha were very upset. When Jesus arrived, he was very sad too. He asked to be taken to where Lazarus was buried.

'Take away the stone,' he said to their amazement. 'Lazarus come out!' he called.

By the wonderful power of Jesus, the Son of God, Lazarus was alive again!

Who were Lazarus' sisters?
Where is the stone that had to be taken away?
Story found in John chapter 11 verses 1-44

Jesus feeds the crowd

Out in the country one day crowds of people were listening to Jesus. By evening they were hungry, but there was no food or shops nearby. Only one little boy had a picnic with him - five small loaves and two small fish.

Jesus said thank you to God for the food and his friends gave it out to the people. Because of Jesus' power everyone had enough. There were even twelve baskets left over!

How many loaves and fishes fed all the people?
How many baskets can you see in this picture?
Story found in John chapter 6 verses 1-13

The woman who was made better

One Sabbath, Jesus was teaching in the church. A lady came in who could not even stand up straight. Her back was bent over. She had suffered for a long time.

Jesus called out to her, 'You are free from your problem.' He touched her and at once she could stand up straight. How she praised God!

What did the lady do when she was cured?
What colour is the lady's dress?
Story found in Luke chapter 13 verses 10-17

The loving father

Jesus told a story about a young man who left home. He wanted to have a good time. When his money ran out, all his friends left him. He had no food and no place to stay.

'It would be better if I were just a servant in my father's house,' he thought. 'I will go home.'

His father saw him coming from a long way off. He ran out to meet him and welcomed him home again.

How did the father show his son how much he loved him?
Can you point to the young man in this picture?
Story found in Luke chapter 15 verses 11-32

The lost sheep

Jesus told this story to show how much he loves and cares for even one person.

A man had one hundred sheep. One day a sheep got lost. The man left all the other sheep safely grazing and went to look for the lost one. He was so happy when he found it. He had a party with his friends to celebrate.

How many sheep did the man have?
How many got lost?
Where is the lamb caught in the picture?
Story found in Luke chapter 15 verses 1-7

The lost coin

Jesus told the story of a woman who had ten precious silver coins. One day one of the coins was lost. She lit the lamp, took her brush and swept every corner of the house. At last she found the missing coin. How pleased she was. She shouted to her friends, 'I have found my lost coin.' They were very happy for her.

Jesus wants us to know that the angels in heaven are so happy when one lost sinner is found by him.

How many coins did the lady have?
Can you see the lost coin in the picture?
Story found in Luke chapter 15 verses 8-10

The one who gave thanks

One day Jesus met ten men on the road. They all were very ill with a bad skin disease. 'Jesus, please make us better,' they called. As they walked along the road they were cured.

One of them, when he saw he was healed, came back to Jesus to thank him. He praised God as loudly as he could. 'What about the other men?' Jesus asked. Only one came to say thank you.

How many were healed?
How many said thank you?
Can you point to the man who said thank you?
Story found in Luke chapter 17 verses 11-19

Zaccheus

Nobody liked Zaccheus the tax collector - he was a cheat. One day Jesus came to town. Zaccheus wanted to see him but he was so small he could not see Jesus over the crowd. He climbed a tree to get a good view. Jesus noticed him and said, 'Come down. I want to come to your house today.'

Zaccheus was so pleased. 'I will pay back all the money I have taken by cheating,' he said. What a difference meeting Jesus made to Zaccheus.

Where did Zaccheus go to see Jesus?
How many children can you see?
Story found in Luke chapter 19 verses 1-10

Children in the temple

Jesus rode into Jerusalem on a donkey. Crowds of people were shouting, 'Hosanna in the Highest.'

When he reached the temple, he healed blind and lame people. The children gathered round and shouted praise to Jesus. 'Hosanna to the Son of David.' Jesus was pleased to hear the children praise him.

What did the children shout out?
What are the children holding in their hands?
Story found in Matthew chapter 21 verses 12-16

On the Cross

Jesus was cruelly treated. All his friends left him. He was taken to a place called Calvary and nailed to a cross of wood. There he died.

Why did this happen? Not just because wicked men hated Jesus. God must punish sin. Jesus took the punishment himself, so that boys and girls who love and trust him can have all their sins forgiven.

Where did Jesus die?
Can you point to the cross in this picture?
Story found in Luke chapter 23 verses 26-49

Empty tomb

Jesus' body was buried in a tomb. A big stone was put at the entrance. Some ladies came early in the morning to see where he had been buried. They found the big stone had been rolled away. Jesus' body was not there! Two angels told them the good news. 'He is not here; he has risen.'

The ladies rushed to tell this good news to Jesus' friends.

Who told the ladies the good news that Jesus had risen?
How many ladies are there in this picture?
Story found in Luke chapter 24 verses 1-12

On the shore

Peter and six friends went out to fish but caught nothing. A man called out to them from the shore, 'Friends, have you any fish?'
'No' they said.
'Throw out your net on the right side of the boat.'

When they did that they caught many fish. One friend realised that the man was Jesus. Peter jumped out of the boat and rushed up the shore to greet him. They all had bread and fish for breakfast.

What did they have for breakfast?
What are the disciples using to catch the fish?
Story found in John chapter 21 verses 1-14

The lame man

One afternoon Peter and John went to the temple to pray. A lame man sat at the gate begging. He asked Peter and John for money.

Peter said, 'I have no silver or gold, but I will give you something else. Rise up and walk!'

He pulled the man to his feet. The man could now walk for the first time. He went into the temple jumping for joy and praising God.

What did the man do after he was healed?
Can you see a little donkey in this picture?
Story found in Acts chapter 3 verses 1-10

Damascus road

Paul went to Damascus, meaning to harm the Christians who lived there. On the road a bright light from heaven flashed round him, blinding him. He fell to the ground. The Lord Jesus spoke to him.

Paul was led in to the town. Ananias was sent to help him. Scales fell from Paul's eyes and he could see again. Paul's life was changed. He loved the Lord Jesus now.

What happened to Paul on the road?
Where is the light in this picture? Is it very bright?
Story found in Acts chapter 9 verses 1-19

Dorcas

Dorcas was good at sewing. She made clothes for poor families. The mothers and children loved her.

Dorcas became ill and died. Her friends were so upset. They sent for Peter and begged him to help.

Peter went to Dorcas' room and prayed to God. 'Get up!' he said. She opened her eyes at once. Her friends were so happy.

What happened to Dorcas?
Are the people in the picture happy or sad?
Story found in Acts chapter 9 verses 36-43

Escape from Prison

Peter was put in prison because he was a Christian. His Christian friends prayed for him.

One night an angel came and woke Peter up. 'Get up quickly' he said. The chains fell off Peter's hands. He followed the angel out to the street, then he went to the house where his friends were praying.

They got such a surprise to see Peter safely out of prison. What an answer to their prayers!

How did Peter get out of prison?
In the picture what are on Peter's hands?
Story found in Acts chapter 12 verses 1-19

Lydia

Lydia was a very busy person. Her work was to sell purple cloth. She loved to go to the riverside to pray with the other women.

One day she heard Paul preaching there, about the Lord Jesus.

She decided to follow Jesus and wanted to do all she could for him. She asked Paul and his friends to stay at her house.

Where did Lydia go to pray?
What is Lydia wearing on her arm in this picture?
Story found in Acts chapter 16 verses 11-15

Paul the preacher

Paul preached the good news about Jesus in many places. He was very brave. He was even put in prison but God sent an earthquake to shake the prison. The prison guard asked Paul, 'What must I do to be saved?'

Paul gave him the only answer, 'Believe in the Lord Jesus and you will be saved.' The prison guard was very happy.

What did Paul tell the guard to do?
What has happened to the wall of the prison?
Story found in Acts chapter 16 verses 25-34

Timothy

Timothy learned parts of the Bible when he was just a young boy. His mother and his grandmother taught him the ways of God. They both loved and trusted God and Timothy learned to do the same.

He became a missionary when he grew up and travelled with his friend Paul - telling people in other lands about the Lord Jesus Christ.

Who taught Timothy about the ways of God?
Can you see Timothy's grandmother in this picture?
Story found in Acts chapter 16 verses 1 -5 and 1 and 2 Timothy